PARROTS

designed and written by Althea
illustrated by Peter Gill

Longman Group USA Inc.

Published in the United States of America by Longman Group USA Inc.
© 1987, 1988 Althea Braithwaite

Originally published in Great Britain in a slightly altered form by Longman Group UK Limited

ISBN: 0-88462-174-X   (library bound)
ISBN: 0-88462-175-8   (paperback)

Printed in the United States of America

88   89   90   10   9   8   7   6   5   4   3   2   1

Library of Congress Cataloging-in-Publication Data

Althea.
  Parrots / designed and written by Althea; illustrated by Peter Gill.
  p.   cm.
  Summary: Describes the physical characteristics, feeding, nesting, and reproduction of this brightly colored bird that lives in hot and rainy mountain forests.
  1. Parrots--Juvenile literature.   [1. Parrots]   I. Gill, Peter, 1924- ill.   II. Title.
QL696.P7A44   1988
598'.71--dc19   88-8510
ISBN 0-88462-174-X   CIP
ISBN 0-88462-175-8 (pbk.)   AC

Notes for parents and teachers

Save Our Wildlife books have been specially written and designed as a simple, yet informative, series of factual nature books for young children.

The illustrations are bright and clear, and children can "read" the pictures while the story is read to them.

The text has been specially set in large type to make it easy for children to follow along or even to read for themselves.

As the sun rises,
parrots call to each other
while they fly to
their feeding area.

The flock leaves the trees
of the forest where they
passed the night.

These parrots live in hot
and rainy mountain forests.
It is dark in the forests and
the trees grow tall to
reach up to the sunlight.
Their top branches open
out like umbrellas.

The parrots feed on the flowers,
fruit and seeds in the treetops.
They are very noisy birds.
Trills, squeaks and calls of
"mee-ya, mee-ya" sound like
people squabbling.

A parrot uses its tongue
and very strong bill
to peel the coat from
the seed or fruit that it
holds and turns in its claw.
The bird eats what it likes,
spitting out the rest.

Male and female birds
are brightly colored.
They molt each year,
growing new feathers
as their old, worn ones
fall out.

After feeding, the flock scatters.
Some birds may fly around in
pairs, perhaps looking for
safe places to nest.
In heavy rain showers, birds
dive for cover in the trees.

When parrots are three or
four years old, they mate and
the female lays eggs.
The two birds will probably
stay together for life.

For a nest, they find
a hole in one of
the large trees.
Sometimes they need
to make the hole bigger
so that they can get in
and out easily.

The female lays two eggs
on the wood dust at the
bottom of the hole.
The eggs are white.
In the deep nest, the eggs
cannot be seen.

The mother bird sits on
the eggs to keep them warm
until they hatch.
The male bird brings her food.

The nest is not safe from
animals like opossums that
eat eggs or young chicks.
It is dangerous for a parrot
to leave her nest
for too long.

After three weeks,
the chicks start to hatch.

The baby bird inside the
egg grows an egg-tooth
on the top of its bill.
It uses the egg-tooth to chip
its way out of the eggshell.
The egg-tooth drops off later.

The female parrot feeds
her chicks on liquid food.
It is made in her crop,
deep down in her throat,
from food she has eaten.
She dribbles this food
into the chick's beak.

While she is looking after the chicks, the male bird goes on feeding her.

After two weeks, the chicks begin
to grow feathers and become stronger.
They venture out of the nesting hole.

The parent birds feed the fledglings
while they learn to fly and
find food for themselves.

Soon, the young birds leave
the nest to live in a flock
with many other parrots.
They feed in the treetops and
roost together at night.

Parrots are found wild in the Americas, Asia, Africa and Australia, but not in Europe. They include parrots like those shown here, as well as macaws, cockatoos and parakeets. Many are familiar as pets, and there is evidence that they were among the first birds tamed. Their ability to mimic sounds and voices makes them especially popular.

The parrots described here have short, stubby tails and are relatively clumsy flyers. They use both their beaks and claws to climb agilely through tree branches in search of food. Their claws differ from those of many birds because two toes face forward, two backward. This makes it possible for the parrot to hold food in one foot while eating; it also increases the bird's ability to climb.

Parrots are hunted for food and captured to sell as pets. For the many parrots that live in tropical rain forests, as in South America, there is an additional danger, the destruction of their natural habitats. There are now laws to stop illegal trade in parrots, and habitats are being set aside for the most endangered species.